D0287363

Volume 3

By
Ra In-Soo
&
Kim Jae-Hwan

Los Angeles • Tokyo • London

Translator - Lauren Na
English Adaptation - R.A. Jones
Retouch and Lettering - Tom Misuraca
Cover Layout - Patrick Hook

Editor - Marco Pavia
Managing Editor - Jill Freshney
Production Coordinator - Antonio DePietro
Production Manager - Jennifer Miller
Art Director - Matt Alford
Editorial Director - Jeremy Ross
VP of Production - Ron Klamert
President & C.O.O. - John Parker
Publisher & C.E.O. - Stuart Levy

Email: editor@TOKYOPOP.com
Come visit us online at www.TOKYOPOP.com

A  Manga

TOKYOPOP Inc.
5900 Wilshire Blvd. Suite 2000
Los Angeles, CA 90036

ISBN: 1-591812-189-4

First TOKYOPOP printing: October 2003

10 9 8 7 6 5 4 3 2 1

Printed in the USA

Story Thus Far

A rift has opened between Hell and Earth, and evil spirits are escaping to the mortal realm. Majeh, a master swordsman in life and an envoy for the King of Hell in death, is being forced to hunt down and destroy these demons before the rift is permanently opened.
Majeh caught Samhuk--a servant for the King of Hell--spying on him and, after making the appropriate threats, now uses Samhuk as his own servant as well.

Despite Majeh's unwillingness to accept the mission, the King of Hell has reunited Majeh's soul with Majeh's body. Majeh's dead body had been perfectly preserved for over three hundred years; immersed in a special hidden lake and guarded by his love, the beautiful Dohwa. Dohwa's proximity to the lake enabled her to watch over Majeh's body through the centuries and, though she could never stray far from the lake, her love for Majeh remained strong and true. Unfortunately, Majeh was re-animated moments too late to save Dohwa from an outlaw who was planning to dump Majeh's body and tap the lake for its miraculous water. Majeh killed the outlaw and only had time for a brief farewell before Dohwa died.

Meanwhile, the three masked men who are responsible for creating the rifts between This World and the Next World continue to plot and scheme. They know that Majeh has been assigned to hunt down the escaped spirits...and that the spirits must kill Majeh first!

FIRST... I HAVE AN APOLOGY FROM THE KING.

HE'S...TRULY SORRY ABOUT TRICKING YOU, MAJEH.

SO, UHM... I'LL DELIVER THE REST OF HIS MESSAGE.

AS I MENTIONED BEFORE, ALL YOU NEED TO DO IS CAPTURE THE DEMONS WHO ESCAPED FROM THE NEXT WORLD AND ARE NOW HIDING WITHIN HUMAN BODIES HERE IN THIS WORLD.

VERY WELL, SAM. I UNDERSTAND!

ALL RIGHT, THEN... LET'S HAVE IT!

...WHAT?

...
A LAW OR A HOLY INSTRUMENT--

.....
.....
WHAT? DON'T TELL ME YOU DON'T HAVE ONE?
UHH... NO...

OW!
UH... UM...
DO YOU HAVE A DEATH WISH?!
YOU BASTARD! WITHOUT A HOLY INSTRUMENT, HOW AM I GOING TO EXTRACT THE DEMONIC SOULS FROM THE HUMAN BODIES?!

THE ESCAPED DEMONS ARE EITHER EVIL OR MALIGNANT SPIRITS... THEREFORE...

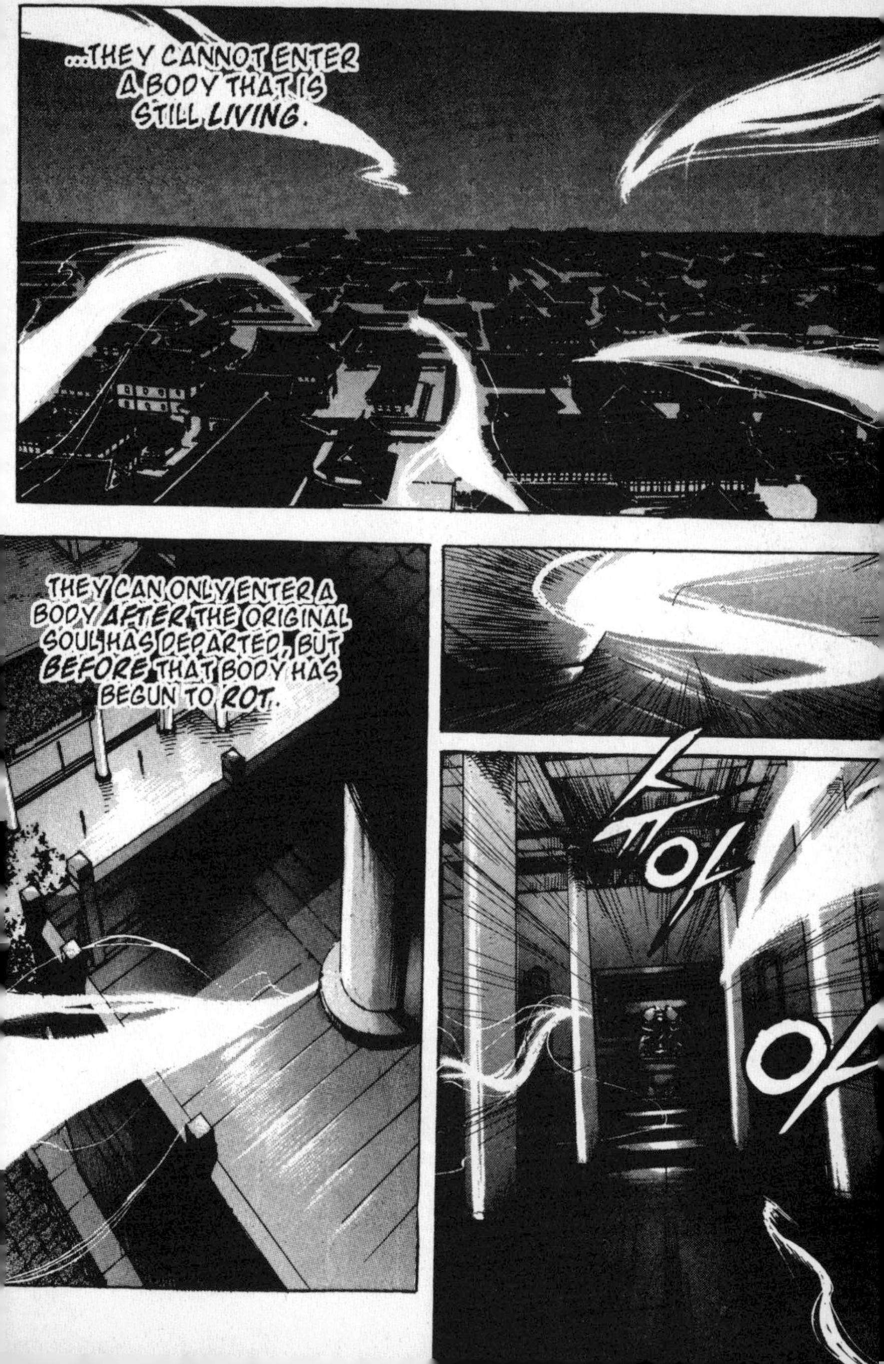

...THEY CANNOT ENTER A BODY THAT IS STILL *LIVING*.

HOWEVER...

...BY NOW THEY'VE PROBABLY FOUND BODIES THAT POSSESS MARTIAL ARTS SKILLS!

WAIT A MINUTE!
HOW CAN YOU BE SO SURE THEY'VE ENTERED THE BODIES OF MARTIAL ARTISTS?

IT'S THE LOGICAL MEANS TO AN END!

HUH?

THERE IS NO DOUBT THAT THEY ESCAPED TO ACCOMPLISH A SPECIFIC GOAL...
AND IN ORDER TO ACHIEVE THAT GOAL, THEY'LL HAVE TO ENTER A BODY THAT ALREADY KNOWS MARTIAL ARTS.

HMM...

EVEN THOUGH THOSE DEMONS MAY BE AT THE PEAK OF THEIR OWN EVIL MARTIAL ARTS SKILLS, THEY CAN'T *EMPLOY* THOSE SKILLS IN A BODY THAT HAS NO MARTIAL ARTS EXPERIENCE!

AND IT'S UNLIKELY THAT THEY'D WANT TO SPEND *YEARS* TRAINING SOME *NOVICE'S* BODY!
MMM...

Y'KNOW, SAM, YOU'RE REALLY SOMETHING. I THOUGHT YOU WERE JUST DUMB, BUT YOU'RE TURNING OUT TO BE...
AT LEAST THAT'S HOW THE *KING* EXPLAINED IT TO *ME*!

...*REALLY* DUMB!

ANYWAY, I UNDERSTAND! I'LL GET RID OF ALL THE ESCAPED DEMONS!

ONE GOOD THING ... IT APPEARS THAT THE CURSE ON MY BODY HAS BEEN LIFTED!
...UM...

BWA HA HA HA HA!
...EXCUSE ME...

WHAT IS IT? WHY DO YOU KEEP BOTHERING ME?
THERE ARE TWO PIECES OF BAD NEWS I HAVE TO TELL YOU.

WHAT ARE THEY?!

IT'S... UH...

......

EH?

WHAT'S... HAPPENING TO ME?!

OH, MY! HOW *PRETTY*!

HOW MUCH *IS* THIS?

HA HA! YOU'VE PICKED ONE AS PRETTY AS YOU! AN EXCELLENT CHOICE, MISS DOHWA!

HA HA! YOU FLATTER ME.

SIR...
WHAT IS THIS THING HERE?

AH, THAT. I FOUND THAT ON THE SIDE OF THE ROAD, LONG AGO. I THOUGHT MAYBE SOMEONE WOULD BUY IT, BUT NO ONE HAS EVER EVEN ASKED ABOUT IT.
HONESTLY... I DON'T KNOW WHAT IT IS.
OH, I SEE.

IN ALL THESE YEARS, YOU'RE THE ONLY PERSON WHO'S EVER SHOWN ANY INTEREST IN IT.

SO... WOULD YOU LIKE TO BUY IT?

IS IT EXPENSIVE?
THAT DEPENDS. FIRST, WOULD YOU MIND GIVING ME YOUR HAND?

MY HAND?

ALL RIGHT...

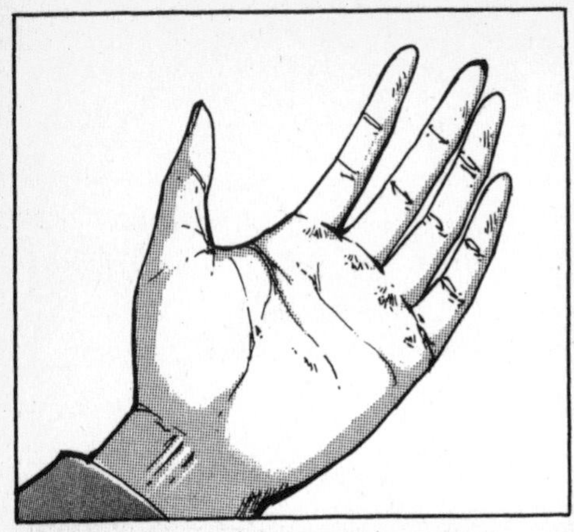

YOU HAVE TINY CALLUSES AT THE BASE OF YOUR FINGERS.

AHHH...! YOU MUST ENJOY EMBROIDERY.

HA HA...! YES, I DO.

ALL RIGHT! JUST PAY ME FOR THE HAIR CLIP AND BOTH ITEMS ARE YOURS!

WOW! REALLY?
THIS IS GREAT!

GOOD LUCK SELLING THE REST OF YOUR ITEMS.
THANK YOU. I HOPE YOU GET HOME SAFELY!
THANK YOU!

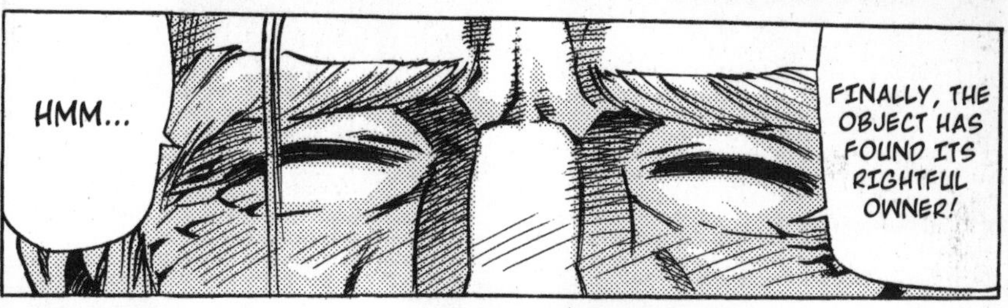
HMM...
FINALLY, THE OBJECT HAS FOUND ITS RIGHTFUL OWNER!

NOW THAT I'VE FINALLY SOLD IT...I THINK IT'S ABOUT TIME I RELOCATED TO ANOTHER PLACE.
BESIDES...

...IN THREE YEARS HERE, THAT HAIR CLIP'S THE ONLY THING I'VE EVER MANAGED TO SELL! I GUESS I'M GETTING TOO OLD FOR THIS...

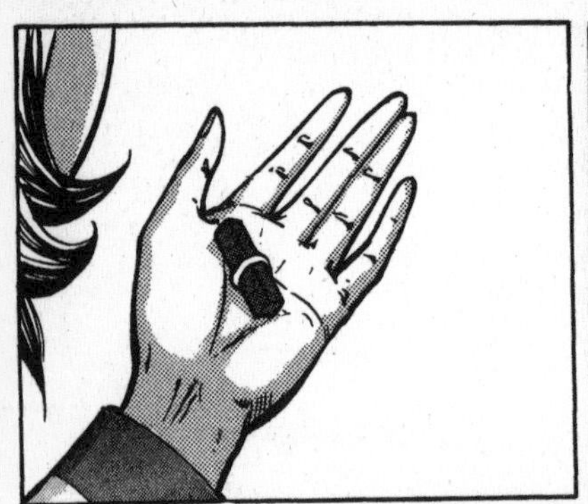

I WONDER JUST WHAT THIS IS?

......

ARE YOU SURE THAT'S HER?

YES, SIR! THAT'S HER!

SHE'S CHANGED HER CLOTHES, BUT WE'RE POSITIVE IT'S HER!
THAT'S RIGHT!

STUPID BITCH! HOW DARE YOU CHALLENGE OUR GANG MEMBERS... I'LL MAKE YOU REGRET IT!
BWHA HA HA HA!

WHY... WHY?!

WHAT'S... HAPPENED TO ME?!

KING OF HELL

WHY IS THIS HAPPENING...?

WHAT'S HAPPENED TO YOU IS JUST THE *FIRST* OF THE TWO BITS OF BAD NEWS I MENTIONED.

WHAT ARE YOU TALKING ABOUT?!
OW!

철푸덕

SOB! IT'S NOT MY FAULT!

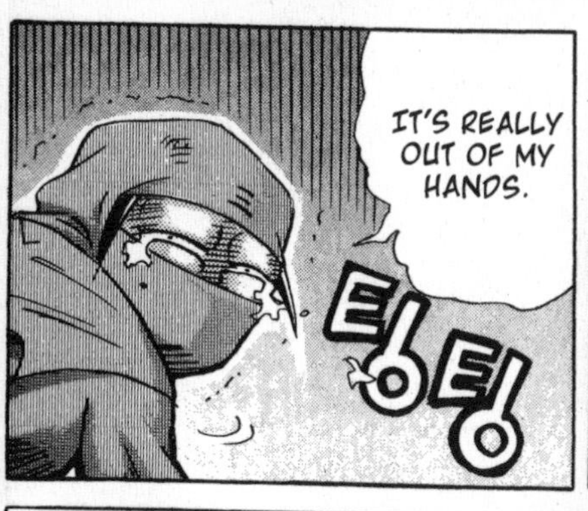

THE IMMENSE POWER OF THE SUPERHUMAN STRENGTH SEALING SYMBOL, ONE OF THE THREE GOLD MARKS OF THE NEXT WORLD, NOT ONLY AFFECTS A DEAD SOUL...BUT A RESURRECTED SOUL AS WELL.

SO YOU'RE SENDING ME ON A SUICIDE MISSION BY TELLING ME TO CHASE AFTER ELITE, DEMONIC FIGHTERS IN THIS BODY!

HOW CRAZY CAN YOU GET?!

AGAIN... THE KING OF HELL SENDS HIS APOLOGIES FOR THIS...BUT YOU CAN STILL RELY ON YOUR ABILITIES...

...!

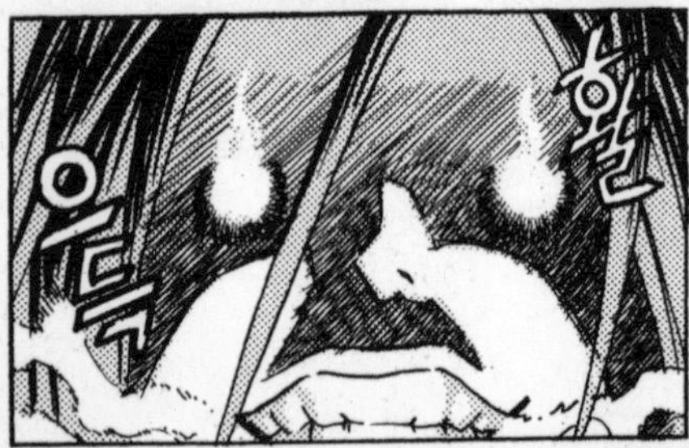

WHAT AM I, YOUR PUNCHING BAG? I GET BEAT UP IN THE NEXT WORLD AND IN THIS WORLD!
OW!

철퍽
WAIT, MAJEH, THERE'S MORE!
MORE?!
깜짝
GASP!
WHAT'S THE SECOND BAD NEWS?
OOOH! I'M AFRAID TO TELL HIM.

YOU'LL BE ABLE TO TRACK THE DEMONS THROUGH THE ENERGY THEY BROUGHT WITH THEM WHEN THEY TRAVELED OVER FROM THE NEXT WORLD...
BUT THE FIENDS WILL ONLY CONTINUE TO GIVE OFF THIS ENERGY FOR A LIMITED TIME, UNTIL THEY'VE ENTERED A HUMAN BODY.
HMM...

THAT ENERGY SIGNATURE WILL DISAPPEAR AFTER ONE MONTH.
AND... AFTER THE MONTH HAS PASSED?
ZIP! KAPUT! ALL TRACE OF THE FIENDS WILL BE GONE!
......
탁

WHAT... WHAT ARE YOU GOING TO DO NOW...
M-MAJEH?
착
퍽
퍽
퍽
I'LL KILL YOU!
YOU THINK I'M GOING TO LET YOU GO ON LIVING AFTER ALL THIS?!

PLEASE, I'M ONLY RELAYING THE KING'S MESSAGE!
팍
IT'S NOT MY FAULT!

. . . . . .
멈칫

HERE, HOLD THIS FOR A SECOND!

. . .
척

LIKE THIS?

YEAH... THAT'S IT.

UHM... OKAY. BUT...
WHY ARE YOU LOOKING AT ME LIKE THAT?

......
헉!

DIE, YOU DAMNED KING!

HOW DARE YOU GIVE ME THIS IMPOSSIBLE TASK??!!
OW!
OUCH!
SAVE ME!

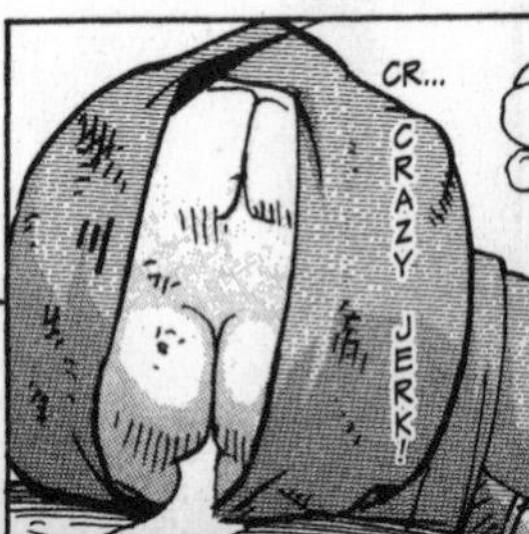
CR...
CRAZY JERK!

YOU THUGS STILL HAVEN'T LEARNED YOUR LESSON...

BUT YOU WILL!

HEHEHE...!

DID YOU THINK WE'D LEAVE YOU ALONE AFTER WHAT YOU DID TO US?
IS THAT WHY YOU BROUGHT ALONG YOUR DADDY?
HOW PITIFUL...

HOW...HOW DARE YOU! THIS IS OUR ELDER COMRADE...
...AND ONE OF THE GREATEST FIGHTERS IN ALL THE LAND!
IT'S JUST LIKE YOU SAID, BOYS, THE LITTLE WITCH HAS LOST HER SENSES!
NOW THAT I'VE ENTERED THE PICTURE, I WARN YOU, I PLAN TO PULVERIZE EVERY BONE IN YOUR BODY!!

YOU CAN'T POSSIBLY BELIEVE...
...THAT THOSE WORDS AND THAT FACE MATCH EACH OTHER?!

MY FACE ...?

WHAT'S WRONG WITH MY FACE...?!

YOUR FACE LOOKS TOO KIND!

REALLY?! THEN I WONDER WHAT KIND OF WORDS WOULD MATCH MY FACE...?
HEY! GET BACK TO BUSINESS!

HAIYAA!
HOW DARE YOU TRY TO CONFUSE MY MIND WITH FRIVOLOUS NONSENSE, GIRL!
FRIVOLOUS?

EXPECT NO MERCY!

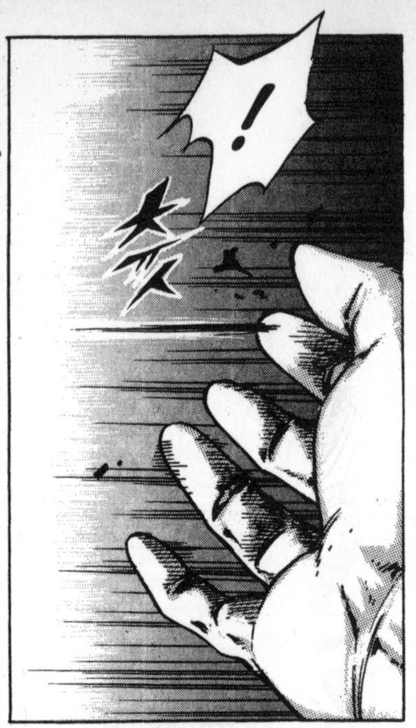
!

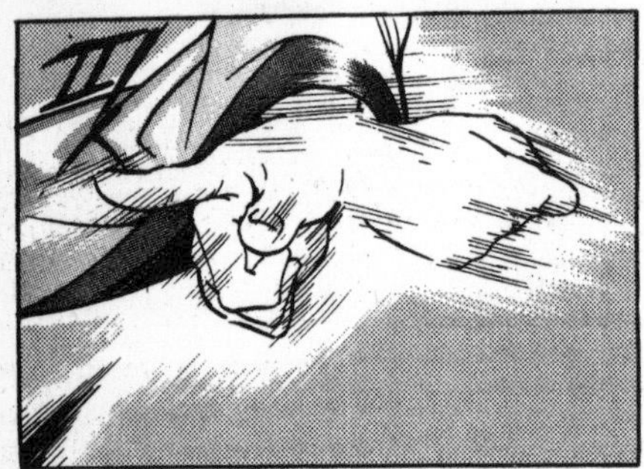

THE...
THE...
!

THE PAIN!
IT'S EXCRUCIATING !!
HUH? IT SHOULD ONLY FEEL LIKE A PIN PRICK...

OWWWW!
YOU... BITCH! YOU USED A POISONED NEEDLE!
NO, I DIDN'T !

SHUT UP! POISON IS THE ONLY EXPLANATION FOR HIM TO BE WRITHING IN AGONY FROM SUCH A TINY NEEDLE!

WHAT ARE YOU TALKING ABOUT? THERE'S NO POISON ON THAT NEEDLE!

HOW DARE YOU USE POISON IN A FAIR FIGHT LIKE THIS...!
A FAIR FIGHT? FOUR AGAINST ONE?
YOU LOOK LIKE A VENOMOUS SNAKE...

...AND YOU ACT LIKE ONE TOO!
ALL YOU KNOW HOW TO DO IS TRICK PEOPLE, YOU WITCH...

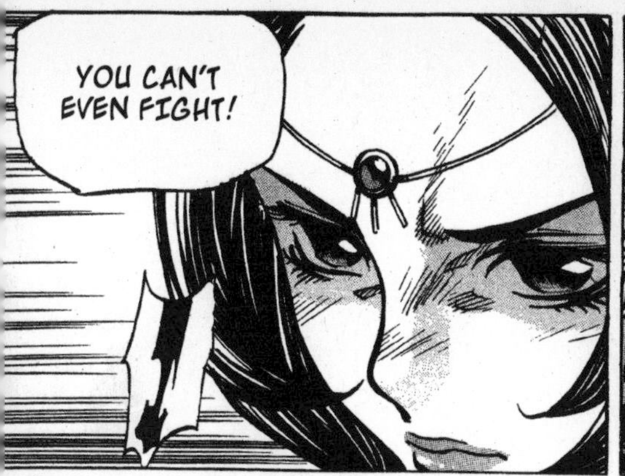
YOU CAN'T EVEN FIGHT!

UHH, GUYS? IT REALLY HURTS!

OH!
HOLD ON! ARE YOU ALL RIGHT?

HA!

I'VE BEEN TOO LENIENT WITH YOU JERKS!

WHAT'S THIS?

WHAT'S THIS LITTLE METAL BALL SUPPOSED TO BE?
HA HA!

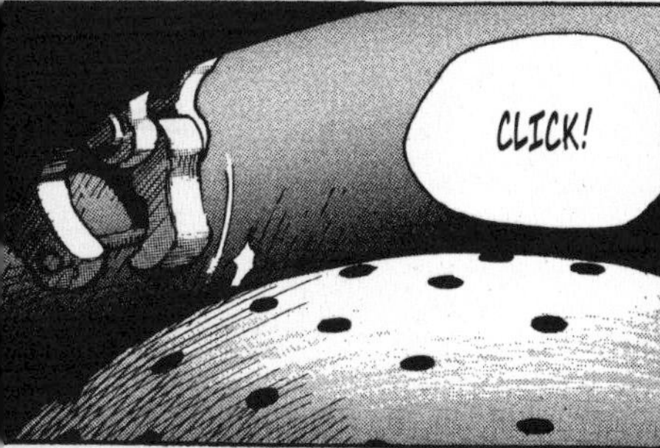
CLICK!

...!
퐁

!!

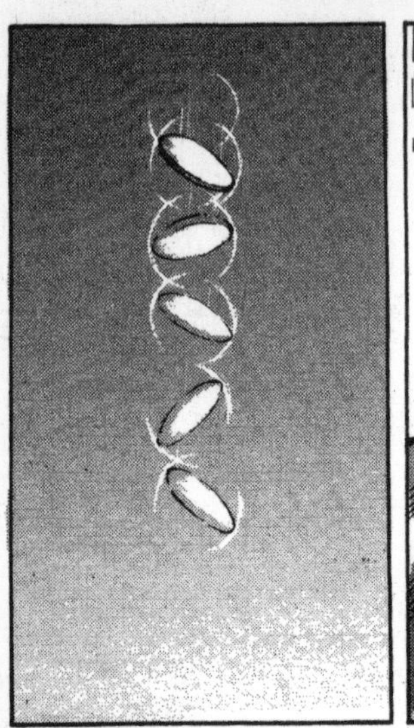

?
톡

팟

피각

철컹
!

HOHO! YOU GUYS ARE SOOOO DEAD.
YOU WITCH! WHAT IS THIS?!
THAT IS THE OOSAJEJOO FAMILY'S POISON CAPSULE!
HOHO!
?
POP!

퍽
AHH...!
팟
퍽

...AHHHHGG!!

PORCUPINES WILL BE CALLING YOU GUYS "BROTHER" FROM NOW ON!
호호

YOU... YOU LOUSY WITCH...!

발라당

IF YOU NEED TO PLACE BLAME, BLAME YOUR OWN PATHETIC SKILLS!

YOUNG LADY? WHY...WHY...
...
바르르르

...DID YOU GET ALL OF US TOO...?
OH MY...

HEHE...!
THERE SHE IS!

EEK!
SHE KILLED ALL THOSE PEOPLE!

THERE'S SOME... MISUNDERSTANDING--
MURDERER!
MURDERER? BUT THEY'RE ONLY SLEEP--
하~
SHUT UP!
...
RUN!
우다다
GET HER!
바바바바

THIS WAY!
DON'T LOSE HER!

LA- LA- LA-

THE CRISP SMELL OF GRASS DRIFTING WITH THE WIND...

I HAVE TO ADMIT, IT'S GREAT TO BE ALIVE!

STOP RIGHT THERE!

GIVE ME EVERYTHING YOU'VE GOT, AND LEAVE IMMEDIATELY!
HUH? AND YOU ARE...?
A BANDIT!
A BANDIT. HMM.
WHAT SHALL I DO...? ALL I'VE GOT IS MY BODY.
SO IN THAT CASE...
TAKE ME!
뽁뽁
부비 부비
웩

...
I'M YOURS!

STOP FOOLING AROUND AND JUST GIVE ME YOUR MONEY!
I TOLD YOU, I DON'T HAVE ANY MONEY!

YOU MIDGET! DO YOU THINK I BELIEVE YOU?!

MI... MIDGET...?!

OH, HE'S... DEFINITELY... GOT A DEATH WISH...

DON'T MAKE ME--

HA HA...! SO, WHAT...ARE YOU GOING...TO DO ABOUT IT...?

바르르

I'LL KILL YOU...

--LAUGH ...?

...!

DEATH . . .

...IS JUST A MOMENT AWAY!

AAA! AAA! SOMEBODY HELP ME! SAVE ME! AAA! AAA! AAAHK!
. . .

SHEESH...

WHAT A COWARD! I WAS ONLY JOKING. I HAD NO INTENTION OF KILLING YOU, STUPID.

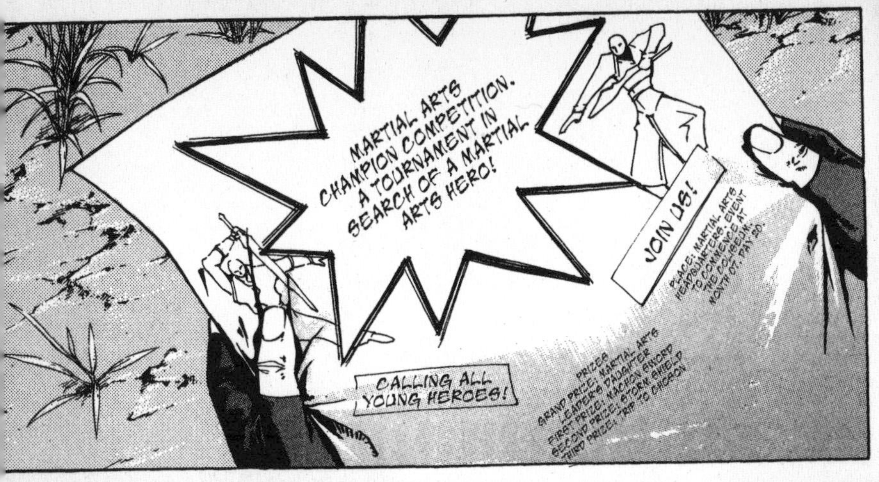
MARTIAL ARTS CHAMPION COMPETITION. A TOURNAMENT IN SEARCH OF A MARTIAL ARTS HERO!
JOIN US!
PLACE: MARTIAL ARTS HEADQUARTERS. EVENT TO COMMENCE AT THE COLISEUM. MONTH 07, DAY 20.
CALLING ALL YOUNG HEROES!
PRIZES
GRAND PRIZE: MARTIAL ARTS LEADER'S DAUGHTER
FIRST PRIZE: MACHON SWORD
SECOND PRIZE: STORM SHIELD
THIRD PRIZE: TRIP TO CHORON
A TOURNAMENT IN SEARCH OF A MARTIAL ARTS HERO?!
WHAT'S THIS...?

KING OF HELL

THE SUN'S BEEN UP FOR AWHILE... AND THEY'RE STILL CHASING ME! PERSISTENT LITTLE BRUTES!

ARTS HERO
I'D BETTER GRAB MY STUFF FROM THE INN AND GET OUT OF THIS TOWN.

MAYBE I SHOULD TAKE THIS OPPORTUNITY TO GO AND SEE THE YONGMOON FALLS?

MARTIAL ARTS CHAMPION COMPETITION. A TOURNAMENT IN SEARCH OF A MARTIAL ARTS HERO!

CALLING ALL YOUNG HEROES!

JOIN US!

PRIZES
GRAND PRIZE: MARTIAL ARTS LEADER'S DAUGHTER
FIRST PRIZE: NACHON SWORD
SECOND PRIZE: STORM SHIELD
THIRD PRIZE: TRIP TO CHOSON

PLACE: MARTIAL ARTS HEADQUARTERS. EVENT TO COMMENCE AT THE COLISEUM. MONTH 07, DAY 20.

I...I'M NOT A COWARD!
AND YOUR BEHAVIOR JUST A MOMENT AGO WOULD BE...?

HUMPH!

YOU RAN AWAY FROM HOME TO BECOME A BANDIT...

THA...THAT'S...

OVER THERE!

I WAS ON MY WAY THERE WHEN MY MONEY RAN OUT.

YOU RAN AWAY FROM HOME FOR THIS?

UH-HUH.

AT ONE TIME... MY FAMILY WAS A RENOWNED MARTIAL ARTS FAMILY IN THE *HOBOOK KINGDOM*.

NOW, THOUGH, EVEN DOGS LAUGH AT OUR FAMILY NAME...

HUMPH! THAT'S WHY I GET ANGRY AT MYSELF!

MY OLDER BROTHER WAS RECOGNIZED FOR HIS SKILLS AND JOINED THE SHAMAN CLAN AS AN APPRENTICE!

I...WASN'T SO SUCCESSFUL!

......

I... I...

BACK THERE, YOU CALLED ME A COWARD!!

I HATE BEING CALLED THAT!!

YES... THIS IS HIM.
MMM...
YOUNG MAN!

COME! ATTACK ME WITH YOUR SWORD!
I'LL STAND PERFECTLY STILL!
HUH?! ...YES, SIR...
척
COME, YOUNG MAN!

UH...UH...
WHY ARE YOU JUST STANDING THERE?! I SAID COME!!

철컹
...
덜덜
으

YOU'RE VERY DIFFERENT FROM YOUR OLDER BROTHER!
!
헐헐
IT WAS SUCH A MINOR CHALLENGE AND YET YOU DROPPED YOUR SWORD. TSK TSK...
THIS CHILD HAS TOO MUCH FEAR IN HIM!

COWARD...
COWARD... I HAVE SO MUCH FEAR...
THIS... CHILD...
N-NO!

YOU'RE... RIGHT...

I WAS... BORN AFRAID!

BUT... BUT EVEN... EVEN I CAN'T STAND MYSELF FOR BEING SUCH A COWARD.

I WAS AFRAID MY PARENTS WERE ASHAMED OF ME...AND I COULDN'T STAND IT ANYMORE!

THAT... THAT'S WHY, AS SOON AS I SAW THAT FLYER, I LEFT HOME!

I...I WAS TRYING TO BE A BANDIT SO I COULD EARN ENOUGH MONEY FOR MY JOURNEY...

......

HA HA...!
I SEE...!

HEY! ARE YOU *THAT* ASHAMED OF BEING AFRAID?

OF...OF COURSE!
HA!
I ONCE KNEW A MAN WHO WAS VERY STRONG...
HE WAS VERY LEVEL-HEADED... WHATEVER THE SITUATION, HE WAS NEVER AFRAID!
...

BUT YOU KNOW WHAT...? WHEN HE WAS A CHILD HE HAD A REPUTATION FOR BEING A COWARD!

...!

BUT HE WAS DETERMINED TO CHANGE THAT!

GRADUALLY, ONE BY ONE, HE OVERCAME ALL THE THINGS THAT HE FEARED...

......

EVEN WHEN HE WAS SO AFRAID THAT TEARS FLOWED... SO AFRAID THAT HE PEED IN HIS TROUSERS...

AND WHEN THERE WAS NO OTHER FEAR TO OVERCOME...

...HE NEVER CLOSED HIS EYES!

...HIS EYES WERE LOOKING DOWN AT THE WHOLE UNIVERSE!

R-REALLY?
YEP!
LISTEN UP!
PEOPLE CONSIDER FEAR TO BE A WEAKNESS...BUT HARNESSING THAT FEAR CAN ONE DAY MAKE YOU A MIGHTY WARRIOR!

KING OF HELL

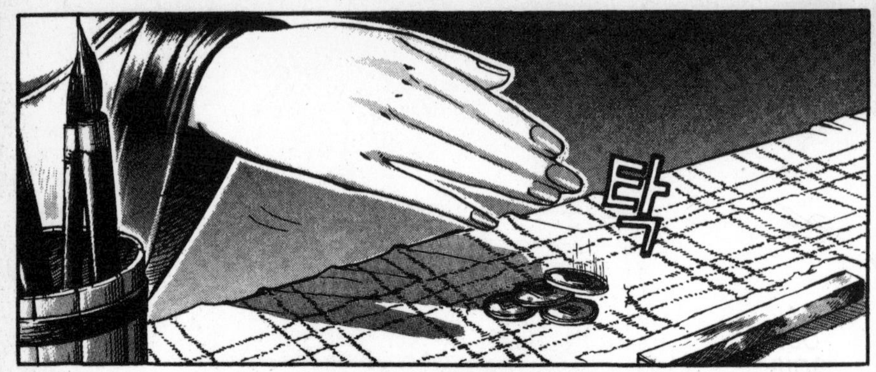
탁

THANK YOU! PLEASE COME AGAIN!

GOODBYE, DOHWA!

AH! A MARTIAL ARTS TOURNAMENT... SOUNDS LIKE FUN!

YOUR NAME...

A...
MIGHTY...
...WHAT IS
IT?

AWESOME!

...WARRIOR...?

YOU RUNT! I ASKED YOU YOUR NAME! CAN'T YOU HEAR...?

HUH?

WHAT YOU SAID, EARLIER...

IT'S TRUE, RIGHT?

HEY!

YOUR NAME?!

I... I'M...

AND YOU?

I'M CHUNG POONG NAMGOONG OF THE PROMINENT NAMGOONG FAMILY!

MAJEH!

MAJEH?!

THAT'S YOUR NAME?

NO...
I FORGOT MY REAL NAME YEARS AGO!

BUT YOU CAN JUST CALL ME "MAJEH."

......

I...I SEE. VERY WELL.

푸드득

UH... MAJEH...?

CAN WE BE FRIENDS?

AHK! ARE YOU CRAZY?!! WHY WOULD I WANT TO BE FRIENDS WITH A COWARD!?
바바바

YOU...YOU DON'T WANT TO BE FRIENDS?
OF COURSE NOT!
AHEM!
LOOK, I'M PLANNING TO GO AND WATCH THAT MARTIAL ARTS TOURNAMENT.
IF YOU WANT TO TAG ALONG, JUST UNTIL WE...
글썽
글썽
...GET... THERE...
살랑

MASTER!
WE'VE SENT THE FLYERS TO ALL THE VARIOUS MARTIAL ARTS CLANS AND PROMINENT MARTIAL ARTS FAMILIES!
HA HA...! WELL DONE. PAY SPECIAL ATTENTION SO THAT THERE ARE NO SNAGS IN THE PLANS, UNTIL THE OPENING CEREMONY!
WE CAN'T DISGRACE THE GOOD NAME OF THE MARTIAL ARTS CHAMPION, NOW CAN WE?!

GOOD. GO NOW.
YES, SIR! AS YOU WISH!

HOW DO YOU THINK THIS YEAR'S COMPETITION WILL TURN OUT?

15 DAYS UNTIL THE TOURN-AMENT.

MR. SECRETARY?!

I BELIEVE...

...THERE WILL BE A VERITABLE PARADE OF YOUNG DRAGONS!

HMM...

YOUNG DRAGONS.

ARE YOU REFERRING TO THE *CHILD PRODIGIES* I'VE HEARD RUMORS ABOUT?

SORIM-- IN THE SOONG MOUNTAINS...

HAAAAA!

팟
팟
!

탁

LAW OF DHARMA !
WRATH OF THE BUDDHA'S DISCIPLE!

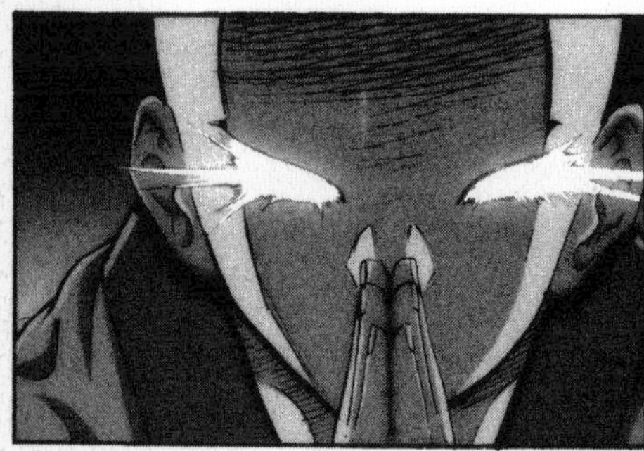

ONE THOUSAND POUND BUDDHA'S DISCIPLE !

!
텅
두두두

SPLAT!

MASTER AT FIGHTING WITH A ROD! DOHAK SAMEE!!
NAME:
DOHAK
AGE:
15
WEAPON OF CHOICE:
ROD
AFFILIATION:
SORIM TEMPLE

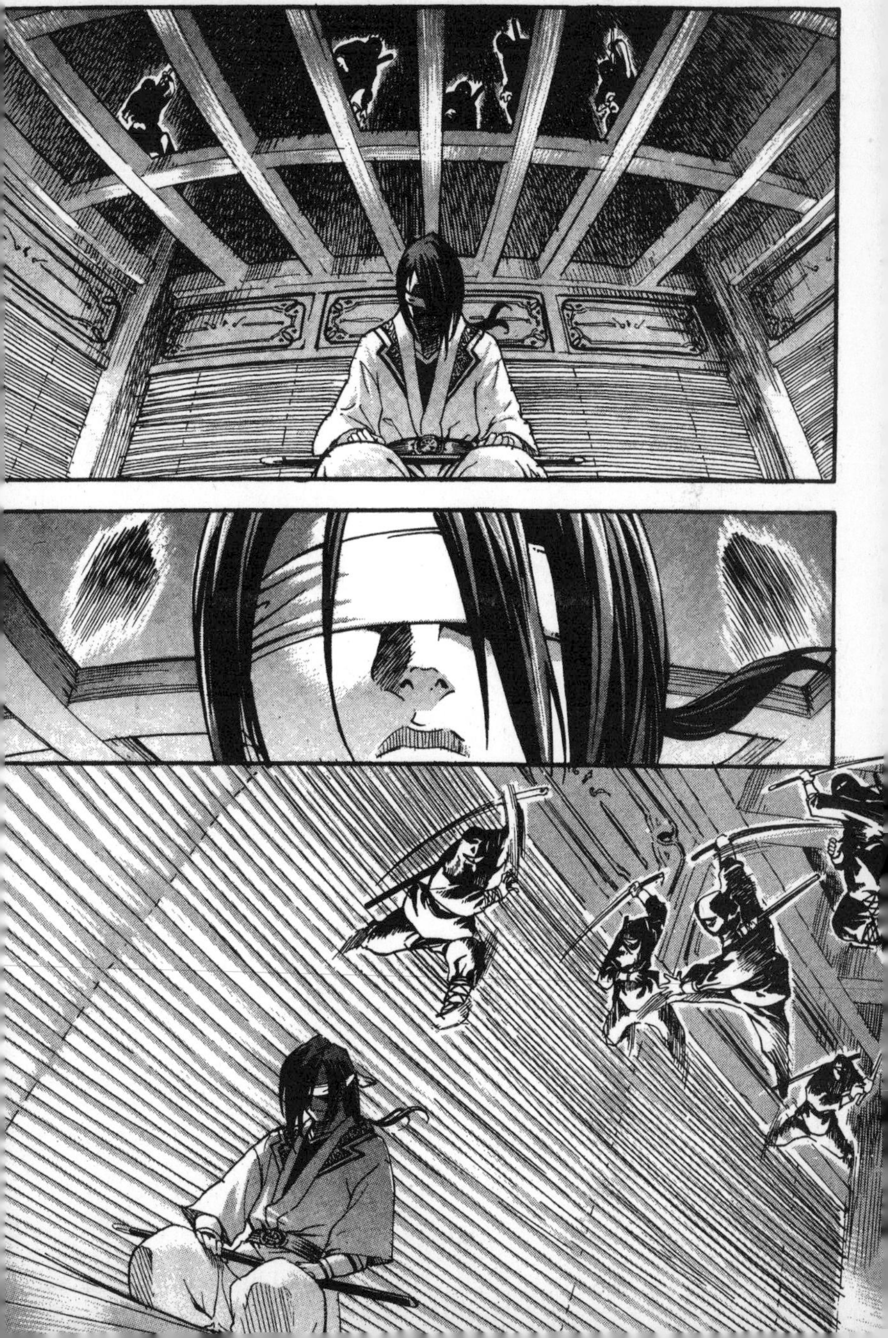

NAME:
YOUNG
AGE:
15
WEAPON OF CHOICE:
SWORD
AFFILIATION:
MOOYOUNG MOON
MOOYOUNG MOON? THAT'S THE FIRST TIME I'VE EVER HEARD OF THEM!
MOOYOUNG MOON IS A SECT WITH OVER 500 ASSASSINS. IT'S A CLAN OF ASSASSINS!
YOU REALLY DON'T KNOW THEM?
HUH-UH...
HMM...

...POONG CHUN!

NAME:
POONG CHUN
AGE:
12
SPECIALTY:
SWORD
AFFILIATION:
SHAMAN

AND IN A REMOTE VILLAGE...

...THE NEXT PRODIGY IS KNOWN AS...

... CRAZY DOG!
NAME: CRAZY DOG
AGE: 6
WEAPON OF CHOICE: CLUB
AFFILIATION: A VILLAGE

LASTLY...

...THERE IS A YOUNG MAN FROM THE BLOOD SECT!

HOWEVER, WE DON'T HAVE ANY INFORMATION REGARDING HIM.
NAME: ?? AGE: 15 SPECIALTY: ?? AFFILIATION: BLOOD SECT
HMM... FIVE PRODIGIES...

I'M REALLY... LOOKING FORWARD TO SEEING THEM FIGHT.

I BELIEVE IT WOULD BE WISE TO SET UP ANOTHER TABLE FOR THE FEAST, MASTER.

ANOTHER TABLE FOR THE FEAST... WHAT ARE YOU TALKING ABOUT?

WE SHOULD SET UP A SEPARATE FEAST JUST FOR THE LITTLE DRAGONS.
A FEAST JUST FOR THE LITTLE DRAGONS...? MR. SECRETARY! IF YOU HAVE SOMETHING ON YOUR MIND, STOP BEATING ABOUT THE BUSH AND SPIT IT OUT...
I'M SUGGESTING THAT WE OPEN A COMPETITION JUST FOR THE YOUTHS!!

KING OF HELL

WE SHOULD HOLD A COMPETITION JUST FOR THE YOUTHS!
MR. SEC-RETARY ...
JUST FOR THE YOUTHS...
...YOU HAVE MY PERMISSION!

까악
까악

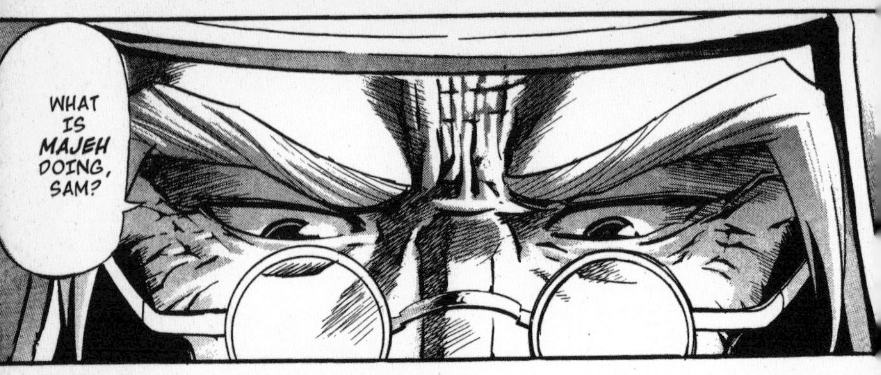
WHAT IS MAJEH DOING, SAM?

HE IS IN PURSUIT OF THE FIENDS.
뚜둑

HOW...HOW CAN YOU SAY SUCH A THING, SIRE...?

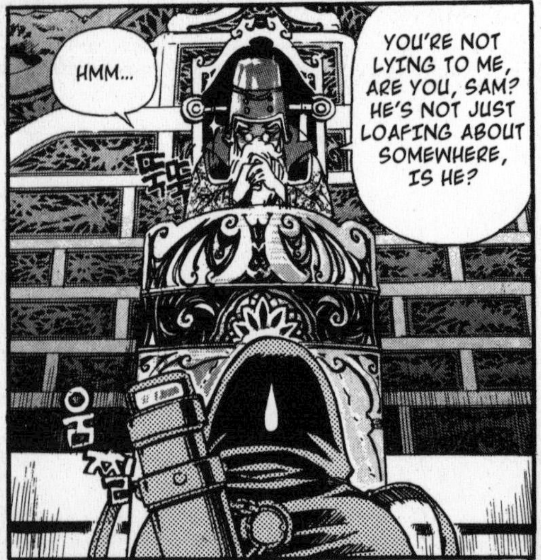
YOU'RE NOT LYING TO ME, ARE YOU, SAM? HE'S NOT JUST LOAFING ABOUT SOMEWHERE, IS HE?
HMM...
움찔

HEE-HEE!
I'M GOING TO GO AND WATCH THE MARTIAL ARTS TOURNAMENT, SAM.
THAT'S AN EXCELLENT IDEA. HA HA!
IF YOU TELL THE KING WHAT I'M DOING, YOU KNOW I'LL KILL YOU, RIGHT?
OF COURSE.
탁 탁
"BETRAYAL MEANS DEATH!" MEMORIZE IT!

방실

DON'T WORRY ABOUT A THING. HAVE FUN AND I'LL SEE YOU WHEN YOU RETURN.

AND YOU'LL HAVE TO TELL ME ALL ABOUT THE COMPETITION WHEN YOU GET BACK!

I FEEL SORRY FOR THIS GUY.

IF BY ANY CHANCE...

...MAJEH ISN'T DOING HIS DUTY, YOU MUST REPORT IT TO ME AT ONCE. DO YOU UNDERSTAND?!

YES, SIRE! AS YOU WISH.
WHAT A PREDICAMENT! I EITHER LIE TO THE KING...

...OR FACE DEATH AT MAJEH'S EVIL HAND!

EH?

WHY ARE MY EARS BURNING? MAYBE SOMEONE'S TALKING BAD ABOUT ME!
POKE

IT'S YOU, ISN'T IT, CHUNG?!
NO... IT ISN'T ME!

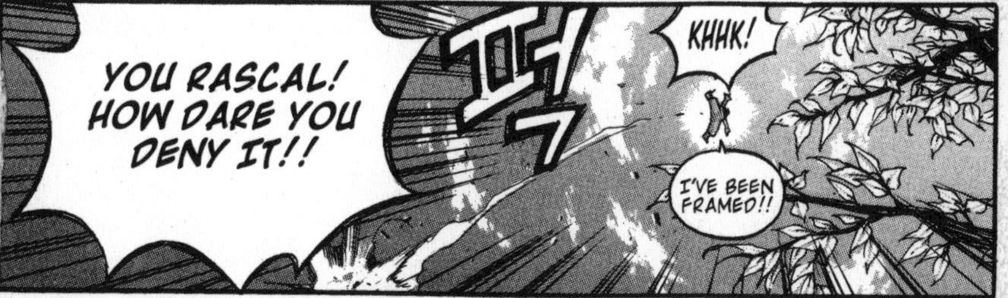
YOU RASCAL! HOW DARE YOU DENY IT!!
KHHK!
I'VE BEEN FRAMED!!

NAKYANG--FIVE DAYS BEFORE THE TOURNAMENT'S OPENING CEREMONY
天香樓

DID YOU HEAR? FOR THIS YEAR'S COMPETITION, THERE'S GOING TO BE A SEPARATE EVENT CALLED THE "LITTLE DRAGON CONTEST!"
LITTLE DRAGON CONTEST?

JEEZ! WHERE HAVE YOU BEEN LATELY?!
우물~

IT'S A MARTIAL ARTS TOURNAMENT JUST FOR THOSE WHO ARE 16 AND UNDER!

WOW! IF THAT'S TRUE, I CAN'T WAIT!

IT WILL BE THE PERFECT OPPORTUNITY TO SEE THOSE CHILD PRODIGIES I'VE HEARD ABOUT!

IT SEEMS LIKE THESE KIDS ARE THE ONLY THING PEOPLE ARE TALKING ABOUT! MAYBE IT'S BECAUSE THE COMPETITION DAY IS STARTING SOON.
홱 홱
?
YOU THINK... SHE SAW US?
안절부절
달달

DON'T EVEN THINK THAT! ANYWAY, OUR DISGUISES ARE PERFECT!

DAMMIT...IF WE KNEW THAT WITCH'S WEAKNESS, OUR STRUGGLES WOULD BE OVER!

AND WHAT ARE YOU GOING TO DO ONCE YOU KNOW THAT WEAKNESS?

WHAT ARE WE GONNA DO?! WE'RE GOING TO GET REVENGE, OF COURSE!

?!

.......!!

♪
OHO! WHAT A SURPRISE TO SEE YOU THREE AGAIN!
UH... WHO ARE YOU?
DO YOU KNOW WHO THIS LADY IS?
NOPE.
...
HAVE YOU GUYS GONE CRAZY? JUST BY LOOKING AT YOU I KNOW YOU GUYS ARE THE INSANE HOUNDS! HOW DARE YOU LIE TO ME! DO YOU GUYS WANT TO DIE?!!
JEEZ! WE'VE BEEN CAUGHT! YOU'RE ABNORMALLY PERCEPTIVE!
....

DOG HIDE! THIS IS A FOOL-PROOF DISGUISE...!
HOW PATHETIC. SO YOU'RE TELLING ME THAT THERE ARE SOME PEOPLE WHO CAN'T SEE THROUGH THAT DOG-HIDE OF A DISGUISE?! TSK TSK...
WOULD YOU LIKE TO ORDER NOW, MASTER INSANE HOUNDS?
. . .
HI!
HA HA HA!
IT'S BEEN A LONG TIME, INSANE HOUNDS! WHAT'S IT BEEN--TEN YEARS? YOU FELLAS STILL LOOK THE SAME. IT WAS NICE SEEING YOU AGAIN!
. . .
WHAT'S UP WITH THIS MANHWA?!

WHERE DID YOU GUYS LEARN SUCH CRUDE DISGUISE SKILLS?

DAMMIT!!!

OH, MY. YOU GUYS LEARNED IT FROM A BOOK?

DISGUISE YOURSELF SO WELL EVEN YOUR DAUGHTER-IN-LAW WON'T RECOGNIZE YOU.

HUH?
THERE'S SOMETHING UNDERNEATH THIS TITLE SHEET.

EH?!

AH, WAIT A MINUTE... THIS EXPLAINS IT!!

WHAT IS IT?
벌떡
띠
ARE YOU GUYS PREPARING FOR YOUR RETIREMENTS?

WHAT ARE YOU TALKING ABOUT? GIVE ME THAT!
DON'T FAINT.

...

DISGUISES SO BAD ONLY YOUR DAUGHTER-IN-LAW WON'T RECOGNIZE YOU. (AN EXCERPT FROM A SENIOR'S GUIDE TO ESCAPING FROM THE HOME.)

SOMEBODY SWINDLED YOU!
쿠당

THAT...THAT BOOKSTORE OWNER! I'M GONNA...
부들
부들
HA HA HA!

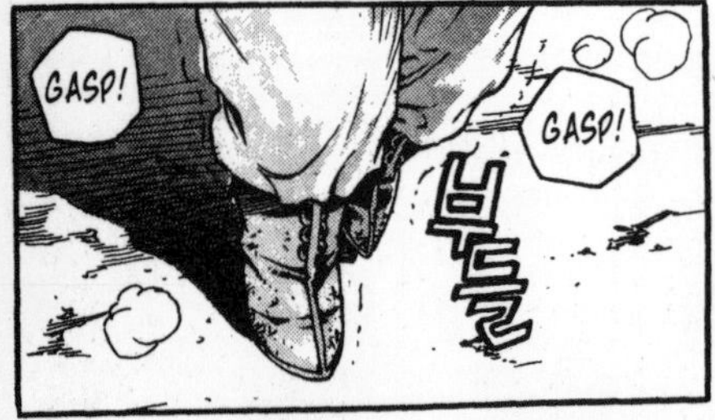
GASP!
GASP!
부드득

WHAT'S UP?! ARE YOU GASPING FOR BREATH JUST BECAUSE OF THAT SHORT JOG?!

WHAT DO YOU MEAN, "SHORT" ?!
WE'VE BEEN RUNNING FOR THE PAST TWO DAYS! I SHOULD BE THE ONE ASKING WHAT'S UP WITH YOU! WHY AREN'T YOU EX-HAUSTED ?!!
SIMPLE... I'VE BEEN USING MY WEIGHTLESS-NESS SKILL.
후비적

HEY, CHUNG POONG, ARE YOU HUNGRY? LET'S EAT BEFORE WE GO ON.
까딱
NO! WHY DO YOU THINK I WAS WILLING TO RUN FOR TWO STRAIGHT DAYS...?

TODAY IS THE LAST DAY TO REGISTER FOR THE COMPETITION!
MAN, BUT I'M HUNGRY! A RESTAURANT IS RIGHT HERE...
LET'S EAT FIRST!
I SAID NO! WE HAVE TO REGISTER FIRST!
GO AHEAD-- RIP MY STOMACH OUT! GO ON! I WANNA EAT FIRST!
YOU THINK I WON'T?!
MOVE, KID!
WHY ARE YOU TWERPS LOITERING IN FRONT OF THE DOOR?
EH?
UGH! BULLIES!

I'M SORRY! PLEASE FORGIVE US!
꾸벅
꾸벅

SORRY?! IDIOT! APOLOGIZING LIKE THAT...

...IN A FIGHT, THE ONE WITH THE LOUDEST MOUTH WINS!
香天
?

WHAT...WHAT... ARE YOU DOING?

HE...CAN'T BE!!

KING OF HELL

EH?

HEY, KID, MOVE ASIDE BEFORE YOU GET HURT!
HUMPH! LOOK AT THIS TWERP.

GET HURT?! ME?
HI~

THAT'S RIGHT!
YOU'RE ASKING FOR IT, KID!!

UH-HUH... I'M ASKING FOR IT, ALL RIGHT.

WHAT ARE YOU GUYS DOING?!

HUH?

IT'S THAT WITCH AGAIN.

PICKING ON YOUNG BOYS... AND YOU CALL YOURSELVES MARTIAL ARTISTS! YOU SHOULD BE ASHAMED OF YOURSELVES!

HA HA! WE WERE JUST PLAYING!

THAT'S RIGHT, THAT'S RIGHT.

IT'S YOUR LUCKY DAY, BOYS!

THAT GIRL... SHE'S THE ONE I SAW THROWING NEEDLES DURING THAT FIGHT AT THE INN THE OTHER DAY!

WE ARE THE INSANE HOUNDS! WE NEVER HARASS LAW-ABIDING CITIZENS.

WHO ARE YOU KIDDING?

THE INSANE HOUNDS... THEY'RE INFAMOUS THROUGHOUT HOBOOK KINGDOM FOR BEING A LITTLE SLOW IN THE HEAD.
IF YOU'LL EXCUSE US, WE'RE IN A HURRY!

THANK YOU FOR HELPING US.
OH, IT WAS NOTHING...

THOSE GUYS ARE THE INSANE HOUNDS...? I COULDN'T **TELL**, WHAT WITH THOSE EXCELLENT DISGUISES!

IT'S PROPER ETIQUETTE. THANK HER!
HEY, WHY ARE YOU THANKING HER? I COULD HAVE HANDLED THEM ALL BY MYSELF!

EVEN IF A CARTLOAD OF THOSE GUYS HAD COME AT ME, I WOULD HAVE BEEN FINE... BUT THANKS, ANYWAY.
HA HA...! WHAT A JOKER.

WE'RE GOING TO BE LATE FOR THE REGISTRATION. LET'S GO.
JEEZ, ALL RIGHT. YOU'RE SO PERSISTENT...

HEY, BOYS, WAIT A MINUTE.
HUH?

ARE YOU BOYS GOING TO REGISTER FOR THE LITTLE DRAGON COMPETITION?

YES. THAT'S RIGHT.

THAT'S GREAT. CAN I GO WITH YOU? I WAS PLANNING ON PARTICIPATING IN THE TOURNAMENT.
I'M SO HUNGRY ...
THEN LET'S GO TOGETHER.

THANKS.
HA HA...! NO PROBLEM.

BY THE WAY, MY NAME IS DOHWA.

THIS IS MY FIRST TIME COMPETING IN THIS TOURNAMENT.
ME TOO.

DOHWA?!

UH-HUH. IS SOMETHING WRONG?

IT'S...IT'S NOTHING.
IT'S JUST THAT YOU HAVE THE SAME NAME AS... SOMEONE I KNEW.

WOW!
SO THIS IS THE MARTIAL ARTS HEADQUARTERS... THE PILLAR OF ALL MARTIAL ARTS.
IT'S MAGNIF-ICENT!
YOU'RE SUCH A COUNTRY BUMPKIN ...!

盟林武

IT'S GLORIOUS!

THERE'S A HORDE OF HUMANS.
OF COURSE.

IT'S BECAUSE IT'S A FORMAL COMPETITION BETWEEN ALL MARTIAL ARTISTS.

AND JUST ENTERING THIS MARTIAL ARTS HEADQUARTERS IS A SOURCE OF PRIDE FOR FAMILIES AND SCHOOLS!

THAT'S TRUE!

IT LOOKS AS IF EVERY PROMINENT MARTIAL ARTS FAMILY BROUGHT ALONG THEIR CHILD, ONCE THEY HEARD OF THE LITTLE DRAGON COMPETITION.

PROMINENT MARTIAL ARTS FAMILY? ALL I SEE IS A GATHERING OF EMPTY CANS.

OKAY, NEXT CONTESTANT.

COMPARED TO THEM, I'M EXTREMELY-- EH...?
O!?

HEY! DON'T IGNORE ME!
YOU'LL SEE THE TRUTH SOON!
LET'S GO!
THEY'RE TAKING REGISTRATIONS OVER THERE.

NAME?

CHUNG POONG NAMGOONG, OF THE PROMINENT NAMGOONG FAMILY.

WH-AAT?!

SAY THAT AGAIN!

탕

THEN IF YOU PLEASE... GO STAND OVER THERE FOR A SIMPLE TEST.

TEST?

ALL RIGHT, IF YOU'LL LOOK TO YOUR RIGHT...

YOU WILL HAVE THREE SECONDS TO PENETRATE THE GRANITE SLABS WITH YOUR BARE HANDS, IN ORDER TO QUALIFY FOR THE COMPETITION!

HA...! HA...!
THEY'RE STARTING.
UNLESS ONE HAS TREMENDOUS CHI, IT WILL BE DIFFICULT TO MAKE AN IMPRESSION ON GRANITE!
HMM...
I SEE YOU'VE COME BACK TO YOUR SENSES.
!
IF I HAD ONLY KNOWN, I WOULD HAVE PRACTICED MORE ON DEVELOPING MY INNER STRENGTH...

I SEE THAT ALL THE USELESS DREGS ARE DROPPING OUT.

DON'T SAY THAT...I FEEL LIKE I'M WATCHING *MYSELF*.

YOU PROBABLY ARE!

ARE YOU **THROUGH** ?!

HOW... HOW OLD ARE YOU?
EHK!

I'M 13 YEARS OLD.

THIS... THIS IS FOR 16 AND YOUNGER...

THANK YOU!
꾸벅
THEN... THEN GO AHEAD!

REALLY. UH, DON'T KNOW HOW TO LIE.
O... OKAY!

AH'M REALLY...
...GOOD AT THESE KINDA THINGS!
AHHK !!

!

HE...HE CRUMBLED THE GRANITE LIKE IT WAS NOTHING...!
하...

WHAT...WHAT TREMENDOUS INNER STRENGTH!

INNER STRENGTH? MORE LIKE *BRUTE* STRENGTH...!

KING OF HELL

I CAN'T BELIEVE THAT'S THE FACE OF A 13-YEAR-OLD...

LOOK... A SNAKE HAND FIGHTER FROM THE BLOOD SECT IS COMING!!

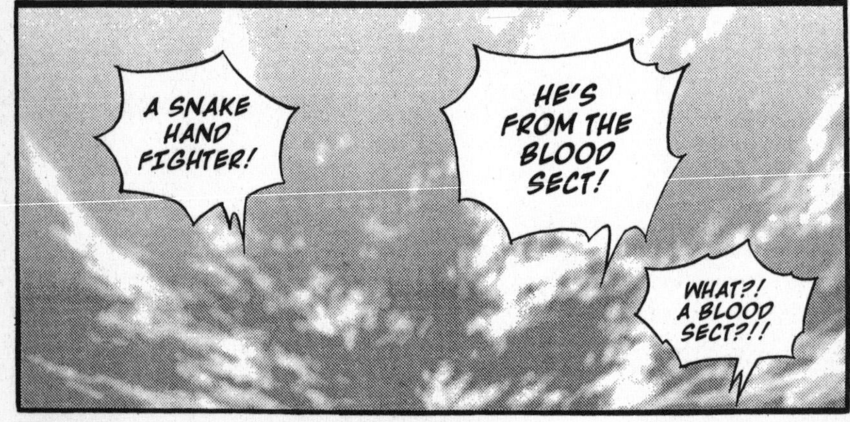
A SNAKE HAND FIGHTER!
HE'S FROM THE BLOOD SECT!
WHAT?! A BLOOD SECT?!!

A BLOOD SECT?

IF IT'S A SNAKE HAND FIGHTER, HE'S DEFINITELY FROM THE BLOOD SECT. THE SNAKE HAND IS ONE OF THE MAJOR TECHNIQUES USED BY ITS MEMBERS.
REALLY? AND IS HE ANOTHER ONE OF THOSE SO-CALLED CHILD PRODIGIES?

MAYBE HE'S THE CHILD PRODIGY WE HEARD THE BLOOD SECT WAS SENDING.
YEAH! IT COULD BE HIM.
HE LOOKS SO YOUNG. IT *MUST* BE HIM!

.....

ALL RIGHT. BEGIN!

OKAY... OKAY...
BLUSH

WHAT IN THE WORLD?! THAT GUY... HE'S BLUSHING LIKE A LITTLE GIRL!

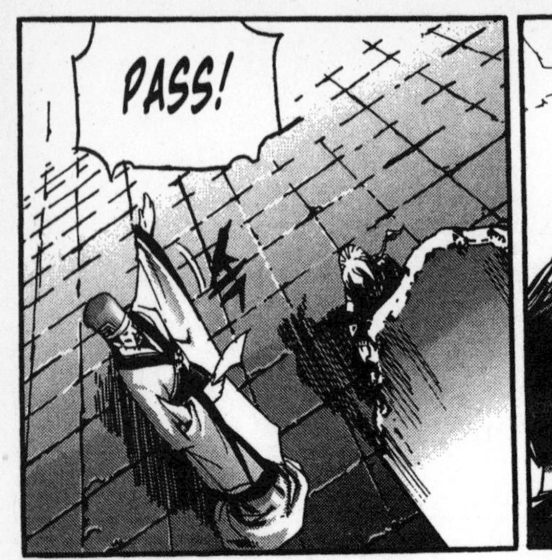
PASS!

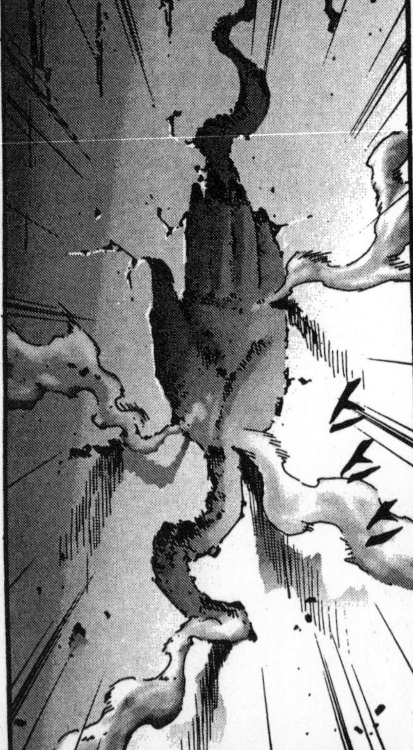

HUMPH!

?

THEY ALL SEEM RELIEVED.

WHAT ARE YOU TALKING ABOUT?

IT'S...BECAUSE OF THE SIZE OF THE SNAKE HAND!
SIZE?!

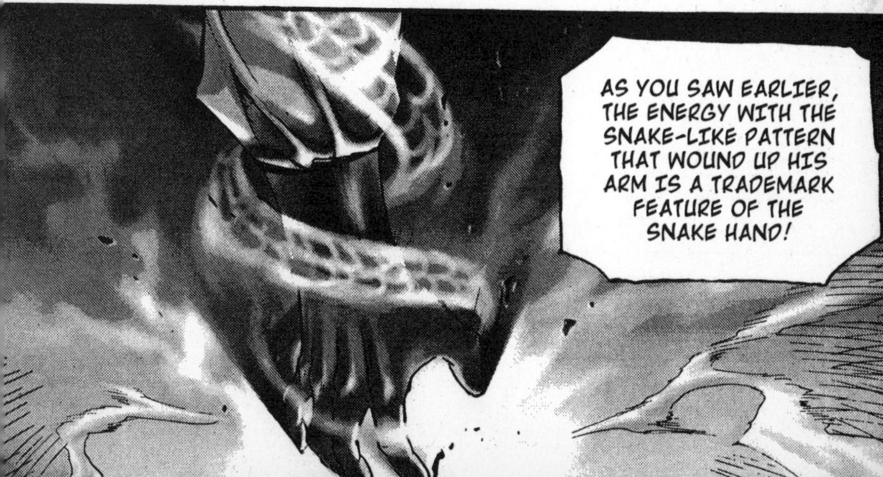
AS YOU SAW EARLIER, THE ENERGY WITH THE SNAKE-LIKE PATTERN THAT WOUND UP HIS ARM IS A TRADEMARK FEATURE OF THE SNAKE HAND!

AND A MAJOR TRAIT OF THE SNAKE HAND TECHNIQUE IS THAT IT ATTACKS THE OPPONENT THROUGH THAT SNAKE-LIKE FORM AND LEAVES A SCAR IN THE SHAPE OF A SERPENT.

SO?

LOOK AT THE DESIGN THE BOY LEFT ON THE GRANITE.

THE SIZE OF THE SNAKE IS SMALL ... PLUS, THE IMPRESSION OF THE SNAKE IS VERY BLURRY!

THAT'S WHY EVERYONE IS RELIEVED!

THEY SAY THAT A ***MASTER*** SNAKE HAND FIGHTER UNLEASHES A DEADLY SNAKE SO LARGE THAT IT LOOKS MORE LIKE A MONSTROUS SERPENT THAN A MERE SNAKE!

IN OTHER WORDS, ALL THEIR CONCERN OVER THE PRODIGY FROM THE BLOOD SECT WAS FOR NOTHING.

WELL...I CERTAINLY CAN'T SEE HIM SCARING ANYONE WITH ***THAT*** FACE.

HE EVEN ACTS LIKE A *GIRL* BY BLUSHING LIKE THAT...
BLUSH

HE'D MAKE A PERFECT FRIEND FOR *YOU*, CHUNG!
...

YOU BASTARD! WHAT DO YOU TAKE ME FOR...?
COME ON!

BOYS, IT'S YOUR TURN NOW.

READY...?

...BEGIN!

YUK-YUK! HEY, YOU'RE GONNA HAVE AN ACCIDENT IF YOU STAND LIKE THAT!
I'M... GONNA KILL YOU!
폼 좋고

HA!

HAI-YAA!

MMM...

FA...

. . .

...PASS!
...

YUK-YUK! WHAT LUCK!
SHUT UP! LUCK CAN BE A SKILL TOO!
AND WHAT ABOUT YOU?! LET'S SEE HOW GOOD YOU ARE!
ALL RIGHT, WATCH CAREFULLY.

THIS IS CHILD'S PLAY... AND YOU'RE CALLING IT A *TEST*?

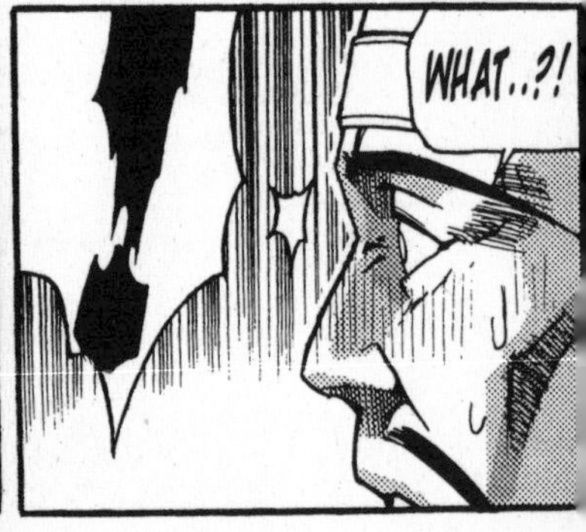
WHAT..?!

......!

CRUMBLE
CRUMBLE
CRUMBLE

HEY, MISTER! IS THIS ENOUGH?

...YES...YES, IT'S MORE THAN ENOUGH!

YOU'VE PASSED!

BWHA HA HA HA! OF COURSE!

THAT BOY... HE'S REALLY **POWERFUL**! AT HIS AGE, HOW...HOW IS IT POSSIBLE?!

HIS **FINGERS**? HE CRUMBLED THE GRANITE WITH HIS BARE **FINGERS**...

!

웅성

...!!

와

KING OF HELL

SO...HAS THE PRODIGY FROM THE BLOOD SECT REGISTERED YET?

YES, SIR. A YOUNG MAN USING THE SNAKE HAND HAS ARRIVED.

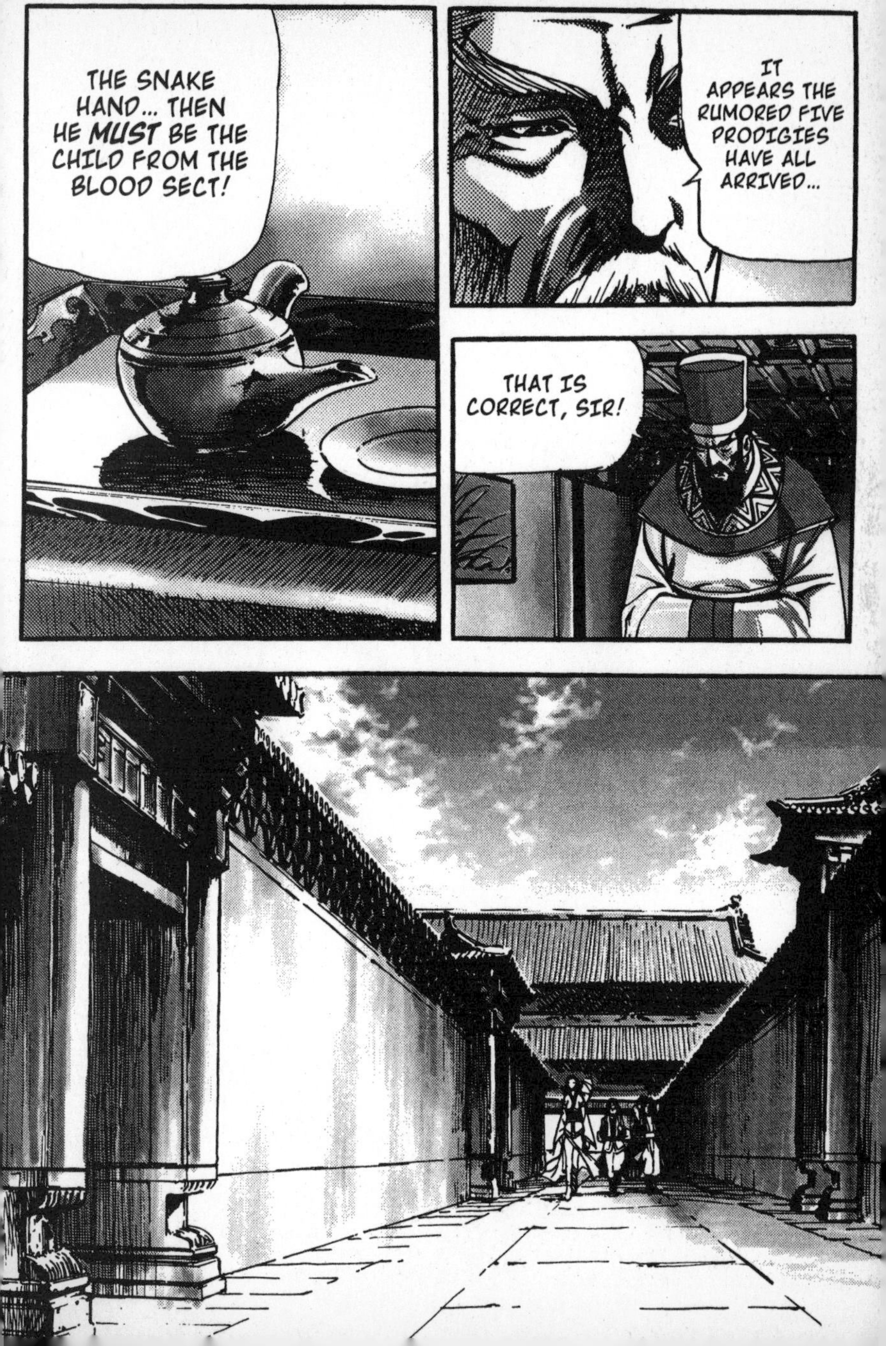

THE SNAKE HAND... THEN HE **MUST** BE THE CHILD FROM THE BLOOD SECT!

IT APPEARS THE RUMORED FIVE PRODIGIES HAVE ALL ARRIVED...

THAT IS CORRECT, SIR!

WHY ARE THE STREETS HERE SO CONFUSING?! THE DAY'S GOING TO BE OVER BY THE TIME WE FIND OUR LODGINGS!
?

AT LEAST WE HAVE A PLACE TO SLEEP. IT'S GREAT THAT THEY'RE PROVIDING IT...

THAT'S RIGHT! AT LEAST IT'S FREE!
YEAH!

CHUNG POONG...

WHY IS THIS *OLD MAID* FOLLOWING US?

YOU'RE NOT, BY ANY CHANCE, TRYING TO SAVE MONEY BY TAGGING ALONG WITH US, ARE YOU?

HO HO!

NO, I'M NOT!

TO BE HONEST WITH YOU, YOU TWO REMIND ME OF MY YOUNGER ***BROTHER*** BACK HOME...

GUYS...

FROM NOW ON, THINK OF ME AS YOUR BIG SISTER!
NO!

AHK!

HUH?

YOU PRACTITIONER OF BLACK MAGIC... YOU SHOULD BE THANKFUL TO BE INCLUDED IN THE COMPETITION.

YOU SHOULD JUST STAY INSIDE YOUR ROOM! HOW DARE YOU WALK ABOUT?!

WHAT ARE YOU DOING?!
THIS IS THE MARTIAL ARTS HEADQUARTERS...
HEY!
HA HA...! LOOK HERE! DON'T GET ALL HYSTERICAL... WE WERE JUST GIVING THE KID A LITTLE WARNING...
HOW DARE YOU ASSAULT A CONTESTANT ON THE GROUNDS OF THE MARTIAL ARTS HEAD-QUARTERS!

HEY! ARE YOU ALL RIGHT?

YES... THANK YOU...

THAT'S WHAT HAPPENS WHEN YOU GO AROUND BLUSHING LIKE A GIRL!

SO...SORRY.
BLUSH
GRRR...

HEY! DO YOU KNOW WHERE THE LODGINGS FOR THE CONTESTANTS ARE LOCATED?
UH-HUH, I KNOW WHERE IT IS. I'LL...I'LL TAKE YOU THERE. FOLLOW ME.
아하
WOW! THAT'S GREAT!

LODGINGS FOR PARTICIPANTS IN THE LITTLE DRAGON COMPETITION

LET'S GO INSIDE. I'M SO EXHAUSTED, I FEEL LIKE I'M GOING TO FAINT.

WHAT ARE YOU DOING?
......
두리번

I DON'T SEE THAT *GIRLY BOY* ANYWHERE...

HUH? WHEN DID HE LEAVE?
HOW TERRIBLE. HE DIDN'T EVEN TELL US THAT HE WAS LEAVING...

. . . . . .

I'M SURE WE'LL SEE HIM AGAIN. LET'S JUST GO IN.
야함

YOU TOO, MAJEH.

WELL, LOOK WHAT WE HAVE HERE!

HA HA HA...!

YOU'VE GOT GUTS SHOWING UP AGAIN, BOY!!
YOU'VE COME BACK FOR MORE SCOLDING, HAVE YOU?
I WAS NEVER SCOLDED... IT WAS "BABY" WHO GOT THE SCOLDING, YOU IDIOTS!

YOU'VE GOT A BIG MOUTH, YOU LITTLE...
...BRAT...!?!

IM... IMPOSSIBLE!!

AAAAAGH!!

SOUNDS LIKE IT'S ABOUT 50 METERS IN THAT DIRECTION.

THAT'S FOR HURTING BABY'S FACE! HA HA...!

VERMIN...

THE MARK OF A SNAKE HAND FIGHTER ...!!

IN THE NEXT VOLUME OF

KING OF HELL

Things are definitely not what they seem at the Martial Arts Championship and, when Majeh, Chung Poong, and Dohwa uncover a trail of deceit and corruption, Majeh becomes the next target for a group of deadly assassins. Surrounded by so many magnificent and ferocious fighters, might even Majeh meet his match?

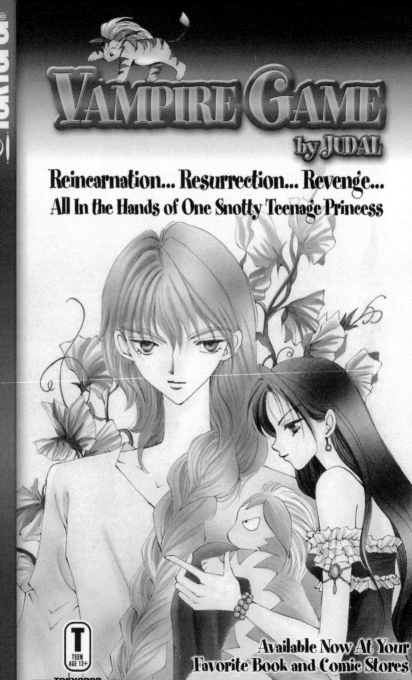